New Frontiers in Dutch Oven Cooking

New Frontiers in Dutch Oven Cooking

Lynn E. Child

&

Susan G. Clendenin

Horizon Publishing
Springville, Utah

This is not an official publication of The Church of Jesus Christ of Latter-day Saints. The opinions and views expressed herein belong solely to the author and do not necessarily represent the opinions or views of Cedar Fort, Inc. Permission for the use of sources, graphics, and photos is also solely the responsibility of the author.

ISBN 13: 978-0-88290-963-9

Published by Horizon Publishers, an imprint of Cedar Fort, Inc.
2373 W. 700 S., Springville, UT 84663
Distributed by Cedar Fort, Inc., www.cedarfort.com

Library of Congress Cataloging-in-Publication Data
Clendenin, Susan.
New frontiers in Dutch oven cooking / Susan Clendenin & Lynn Child.
p. cm.
ISBN 978-0-88290-963-9 (acid-free paper)
1. Dutch oven cookery. I. Child, Lynn, 1948- II. Title.
TX840.D88C54 2009
641.5'89--dc22
                        2009006040

Cover design by Angela D. Olsen
Cover design © 2009 by Lyle Mortimer
Edited and typeset by Natalie A. Hepworth

Printed in the United States of America

10 9 8 7 6 5 4 3 2 1

Printed on acid-free paper

Dedication

We would like to dedicate this book to our parents Eldon E. and Leona E. Butler Child. They always told us children that we could do anything we wanted to if we wanted to do it bad enough. Mom is the one who taught us all how to cook. They were the parents of eight children—six girls and two boys. She always said that anything her girls could do, her boys could do, and anything her boys could do, her girls could do. So we were raised to know that we could do anything. We all love you Mom and Dad, and we all miss you both.

Leona E. Butler Child
1922–1990

Eldon E. Child
1920–1970

Contents

Chapter 3

Chapter 4

Chapter 5

CHAPTER 6
ONE POT MEALS—

CHAPTER 7

Chapter 8
Side Dishes—

ACKNOWLeDGMeNtS

We would like to say thanks to our cousin Brad Probst for telling us to write this book. Also for having the faith in us to be able to write it. Thank you for having faith.

I am careful of the words I say,
To keep them soft and sweet . . .
I never know from day to day
Which ones I'll have to eat!

Introduction

Let's look back to when the pioneers came across the plains. What did they cook in? Dutch ovens. They may have called them "the old black pot" or "the iron pot." But whatever they called them, it was still a Dutch oven. Dutch ovens are really fun to cook in. No matter how easy or how hard a recipe is, everything turns out great.

When the pioneers used Dutch ovens, most of the recipes were simple because they didn't have the spices or some of the other ingredients we have today. The pioneers had to make everything from scratch, like bread and pastries. Now we have frozen bread dough and ready-made pastry. All we have to do is go to the store and buy a package or can of whatever we need.

It took the pioneers a lot longer to cook their meals than it takes us now, even in Dutch ovens. Sometimes, they even had to let their meals cook in the fire all day. It doesn't take that long anymore!

We encourage you to try as many recipes in this book as you can. You will have fun and want to cook in your Dutch oven more and more. It is also fun to come up with your own recipes or just change a few things in these recipes to make them your own. The best part is trying your own recipes and having them come out like you cooked them in your own kitchen. Dutch oven cooking is not just for camping. You can cook in your Dutch oven in your backyard, the park, or any place where you can set it up.

Dutch Oven Names

Some call them iron pots,
Some call them black pots,
Some call them cast iron pots,
But whatever you call them
They are still Dutch ovens
And food turns out great!

DUtCH OVeN

THE BEST WAY TO COOK!

HELPFUL HINTS

1. Grease Dutch ovens each time you use them. If you line the Dutch oven with foil it is not as important to grease it. But you can if you would like to will help the foil from not sticking as much or as badly. It does not matter what you use. You can use a cooking spray, shortening, or a little oil. Remember you need just a little of whatever you use.

2. Try to find a hard plastic scraper. It will make your cleanup go a lot faster and easier, but you can use a green scrub pad or a heavier one if you need it.

3. If you use too much spray or oil when lining your Dutch oven it could stick. The foil can be taken out in one piece but you can't lift it out. You need to be very careful and pull it up slowly. If you see that you have a lot of oil in one spot before you line it take a paper towel and wipe it out, remember you want just a very light coat. It might need to be warmed up a little to wipe out the extra oil.

4. Use a thin coat of oil after cleaning so the Dutch oven will not rust. Too much oil could cause a rancid smell.

5. As you store for winter, try a paper towel inside the Dutch oven to help stop the moisture from collecting. This is one way to avoid rust in your Dutch oven. You can also put a paper towel in after each time you use it if you don't know when you are going to use it again.

6. To bring out the flavor of the Dutch oven, use bay leaves in your dishes. Remove the leaf after cooking and before serving. Just put 1 or 2 bay leaves in; basil flakes work also, just a teaspoon or two.

PREPACKING FOR OUTINGS

For camping or an outing, prepack all your dry ingredients. You can combine all the dry ingredients into one ziplock bag, or put each ingredient in a separate bag. Make sure you label each ingredient, including how much is in the bag and what recipe it is for. Remember to take along the other ingredients you will need, like eggs, water, oil, and so forth. Most important, don't forget the recipe! Prepacking your ingredients will save time and space. This will also prevent you from making last-minute trips to the store for something you forgot. Also, you won't have to skip out on a dish because you forgot to take something with you. It is also helpful to put all your ingredients and the recipe in one large bag so everything you need is in one place.

You can also do some prep work for the ingredients in your recipe. If the recipe calls for onions, green peppers, carrots, apples, or any other vegetable or fruit, cut them up at home and put them in ziplock bags to save prep time later on. You can also cut your meat ahead of time and either put it in the cooler right away or freeze it until you are ready to take it with you. Be careful if you do this, as frozen meat isn't very easy to cut.

DUTCH OVEN TOOLS

*   DUTCH OVENS—Buy the size you will use most often for the dishes you want to make.
*   LID LIFTER—Use this to lift a hot lid off your Dutch oven.
*   GLOVES—Buy heavy gloves, preferably leather, so you can carry the hot Dutch oven or drain liquid as needed.
*   TONGS—Buy a pair of long tongs to use when you place coals under and on top of the Dutch oven. You may want to buy more than one pair so you can also use them to turn meats.
*   LONG-HANDLED SPOONS AND FORKS—These are useful when stirring and serving your food.
*   COOKING SPRAY OR SHORTENING—Use these to treat your Dutch oven.
*   PAPER TOWELS—Use paper towels to wipe your Dutch oven clean

HOW TO...

CARING FOR YOUR DUTCH OVEN

CURING YOUR DUTCH OVEN

Place your Dutch oven in a sink full of very hot water—as hot as you can get it. Let it soak for a few minutes and then add a little bit of dish soap. Then get a stiff brush or a harsh scrubber pad. Make sure you get all the wax preservative off. Rinse the Dutch oven, making sure to get all the dish soap out. Dry with paper towels then let air dry for a while. After the Dutch oven is dry, put a good coat of shortening all over the Dutch oven. Place tin foil on the bottom rack of your oven and preheat to 350 degrees. Put your Dutch oven upside down in the oven for one hour. Let cool completely before removing.

A barbecue grill also works as a heat source for curing your Dutch oven. You might have to remove the grills in order to put the Dutch oven inside, upside down. This takes about the same amount of time as it does in an oven.

Remember to be very careful any time you handle a hot Dutch oven. Whether you are curing or cooking, use the right tools.

Some Dutch ovens come already seasoned. You can purchase these in almost any hardware store or from any Dutch oven dealer. There are also special cleaning solutions and conditioners for Dutch ovens. Again, you can find these almost anywhere Dutch ovens are sold.

CLEANING

Put hot water and a little soap in your Dutch oven and let it soak for a while. After it soaks for a while, get a hard plastic scraper to remove all the stuck-on food. Rinse your Dutch oven well and wipe dry with paper towels. Make sure to dry your Dutch oven thoroughly. It sometimes helps to put it in the oven for 5 minutes or so to get all the excess moisture out. After your Dutch oven is completely dry, use a paper towel with shortening or oil on it to lightly coat the Dutch oven. If the coat of shortening or oil is too thick, you will get a rancid smell after a while. However, if you don't coat it at all, your Dutch oven might rust. If you don't know when you are going to use your Dutch oven next, store it with a paper towel inside to absorb any excess moisture.

Using a heavy duty scrub brush or scraper will not hurt your Dutch oven. However, be careful not to remove all the dark coating. The darker your Dutch oven is, the better cured it is. Just make sure you have *all* the soap rinsed off the Dutch oven before you coat it in shortening or oil. Remember, the darker your Dutch oven is, the better cured it is.

Cooking with Bottom Heat

There might be times when you will not be able to use charcoals. What can you do? Don't worry! Many dishes can be cooked with bottom heat only.

Your regular outdoor camping stove can be used with your Dutch oven. Use the Dutch oven just like you would a pot on your home stove. Be careful not to let the Dutch oven get too hot. Just remember that cast iron holds heat more than the pans you use in your kitchen at home. The heat on the bottom of the Dutch oven does not have to be very high to cook the food.

Many dishes can be cooked with just bottom heat. You can make soups, stews, breakfast foods, some meat dishes, and many other main and side dishes. If you can cook it on top of your stove, you can cook it in your Dutch oven with just bottom heat. Breads and desserts should not be cooked with bottom heat only unless you have a Dutch cap. More information about the Dutch cap is given below.

Remember, if you go some place and find that you either can't use charcoal, or don't have any at all, you can still make a great meal in your Dutch oven.

Dutch Cap

The Dutch Cap is a cap that fits down over the Dutch oven. It makes cooking in your Dutch oven just like cooking in your conventional oven at home. A Dutch cap allows you to have both top and bottom heat when charcoals aren't available.

The Dutch cap has a vent on top that helps the heat escape so you don't have too much heat around the Dutch oven. It is better to start out with the vent all the way open, and then if you think you need more heat, close the vent a little at a time so you don't overheat your food. The Dutch cap is a close fit to the 12-inch Dutch oven and this is the biggest Dutch oven you can use the cap with.

With an outdoor stove and the Dutch cap you can cook anything you want to. The flame on the outdoor stove only needs to be about ¼ to ½ of an inch high. Don't go over ¾ inches. If the heat is too high on the bottom, your food will burn, so watch the heat very closely. Your food will also burn if there is too much heat around the Dutch oven, so keep the vent on the Dutch cap as open as you can. This will help so the food will not burn. The Dutch cap also makes it possible to cook breads and desserts when only a bottom heat source is available.

Eliminating a Rancid Smell

If you do end up with a rancid smell in your Dutch oven, you need to get all the excess oil out of it. Heat your Dutch oven, then carefully wipe out all the old oil. If the smell is still there, try washing it in very hot water, letting it soak for a while. Then wash it as you normally would, with soap and a scrub brush. After you get all of the old oil off the Dutch oven it will need to be re-cured.

If you clean the Dutch oven but don't clean the lid, the lid could get rusty and cause a rancid smell. If you wash and treat your Dutch oven and the smell is still there, it might be your lid. Always clean your lid and treat it with oil just as carefully as you do your Dutch oven.

Eliminating Rust

If your Dutch oven gets rust in it, you must remove all the rust before you use it. Use soap, hot water, and a scrubbing pad, like an SOS pad, to get all the rust out of the Dutch oven. There is a clothlike sandpaper for metal called an emmer cloth that is really useful when removing rust from your Dutch oven. You might have to scrub off some or all of the black coating to remove all the rust—just be careful not to remove too much. Rinse the Dutch oven well after removing the rust, and dry it thoroughly. It sometimes helps to put your Dutch oven in a warm oven for a few minutes to remove any excess moisture. After your Dutch oven is dry, treat with shortening or oil.

It is also good to treat the outside of your Dutch oven with short-ening or oil. This will cure the outside and make it look better. The outside is just important as the inside. Always remember to clean the lid of your Dutch oven when cleaning the oven itself.

BreaKFast

Start Your Day Off Right!

Any of these delicious breakfast recipes can be made into breakfast burritos. Spice up your dishes by adding chili peppers, salsa, hot peppers, or other spices you like. You can add anything you want, really.

When cooking any of these breakfast dishes, remember that the top heat does not have to be used. All these recipes will cook just fine with bottom heat only. However, we have added the instructions for using top coals in a couple of the recipes.

Remember, breakfast is the meal that starts your day, so make it a good one!

★ High Uinta Breakfast ★

1 lb. bacon, cut into 1-inch pieces
½ medium onion, chopped
½ medium green bell pepper, chopped
1 lb. ham, diced
1 (2 lb.) bag southern-style hash browns
salt and pepper to taste
¼ tsp. garlic powder
12 eggs, well beaten
1 lb. cheddar cheese, grated
1 jar salsa, any kind (optional)

PREHEAT a 12-inch Dutch oven to 350 degrees, using bottom coals only. Cook bacon, remove, and place on paper towels to remove excess grease. Drain grease from Dutch oven, leaving about 1 teaspoon to sauté vegetables in. Add onions and green peppers and sauté until tender. Add bacon back in, and add ham. Stir well. Add hash browns and seasoning, and stir. Make sure that the meat and vegetables get mixed with the hash browns. Add top coals and cook until potatoes are golden brown. Add eggs and cook until firm. You can either leave the eggs on top or stir them in with the meat and vegetables. Add cheese and heat until cheese is melted.

DUTCH OVEN SIZE: 12"
TOTAL COOKING TIME: about 45 minutes
TOTAL COALS: 24
TOP COALS: 14
BOTTOM COALS: 10

★ For variety add sausage, try just one meat, or try all three meats. If you try all three meats, just add about ½ pound of each. You can also add mushrooms or any other vegetables you choose.

★ Ham and Cheese Scramble ★

½ medium onion, chopped
½ medium green bell pepper, chopped
1 lb. ham, diced
12 eggs, well beaten
⅔ cup milk
salt and pepper to taste
3 cups cheese, grated

PREHEAT 10-inch Dutch oven to 350 degrees, using bottom coals only. Add a small amount of oil and sauté onions and green peppers until tender. Add ham and stir. Beat eggs and milk, season, and add to ham and vegetables. Cook until eggs are firm. Add cheese and heat until melted. Stir eggs a few times so they will not burn.

DUTCH OVEN SIZE: 10"
TOTAL COALS: 10 (bottom coals only)

★ Add anything else you would like. This mixture makes great burritos!

★ Scrambled Eggs ★

6–12 eggs, well beaten (add more eggs if desired)
½–1 cup milk
4 Tbsp. butter
season to taste

PREHEAT 8-inch Dutch oven to 350 degrees, using bottom coals only. Beat eggs and add milk. In Dutch oven, melt butter. Add eggs and cook until firm. Use a long-handled spatula to keep the eggs stirred so they will not stick to the Dutch oven or burn. If you'd like, you can use a cast iron frying pan instead of the Dutch oven.

DUTCH OVEN SIZE: 8"
TOTAL COALS: 6–8 (bottom coals only)

★ Vegetable Scramble ★

½ medium onion, chopped
½ medium green bell pepper, chopped
1 (8 oz.) can mushrooms, drained (sliced or whole)
vegetables (any kind)
12 eggs, well beaten
⅔ cup milk
salt and pepper to taste
2 cups cheese (any kind), grated

PREHEAT 10-inch Dutch oven to 350 degrees, using bottom coals only. Add a small amount of oil and sauté onions, green peppers, and any other vegetables you choose until tender. In a separate bowl, combine eggs, milk, salt and pepper. Beat well. Pour egg mixture into Dutch oven and mix well. Stir often so the eggs do not stick or burn. Cook until firm and then add cheese and heat until melted.

DUTCH OVEN SIZE: 10"
TOTAL COALS: 10 (bottom coals only)

★ Add green chilies or jalapeños for a spicier dish.

★ ALL Meat Scramble ★

½ lb. ham, diced
½ lb. sausage, cut up or chopped
½ lb. bacon, cut into 1-inch pieces
1 medium onion, chopped
1 medium green bell pepper, chopped
1 (8 oz.) can mushrooms, drained
12 eggs, well beaten
⅔ cup milk
¼ tsp. garlic powder
salt and pepper to taste

PREHEAT 10-inch Dutch oven to 350 degrees, using bottom coals only. Cook meats and remove from Dutch oven. Place meats on paper towels to remove excess grease. Drain grease from Dutch oven, leaving about 1 teaspoon to sauté vegetables. Add onion and green bell pepper, and sauté until tender. Add meat back into the Dutch oven and mix well. Add mushrooms. In a separate bowl, add eggs, milk, and seasoning. Beat well and add egg mixture to meat. Stir well and place lid back on Dutch oven. Stir often so the eggs do not stick or burn. Cook until eggs are firm.

DUTCH OVEN SIZE: 10"
TOTAL COALS: 8–10 (bottom coals only)

½ lb. bacon, cut into 1-inch strips
½ medium onion, chopped
½–1 cube butter
1–1½ lbs. hash browns
6 eggs
1 (6 oz.) sour cream
1 tsp. chili powder
½ tsp. garlic (optional)
1 tsp. garlic salt
½–1 cup milk
1 cup cheese, shredded

Cook bacon and remove from Dutch oven. Drain grease, leaving a couple of spoonfuls. In the remaining bacon grease, sauté onions until tender. Remove onions and set aside. Add ½ cube of butter to the Dutch oven and cook hash browns. When hash browns are done, add the bacon and onions and mix well. In a separate bowl, scramble eggs and add sour cream, chili powder, garlic, garlic salt, milk, and cheese. Pour egg mixture over the hash browns and bacon and stir well. Let eggs cook until firm. More cheese can be added to the top if you would like. This recipe can be done in a cast iron skillet, cast iron wok, or Dutch oven.

Dutch oven size: 10"
Total coals: 10 (bottom coals only)

★ POLISH Sausage and Eggs ★

1 pkg. (16 oz.) Polish sausage, sliced into ½-inch slices
½ cube butter
1 pkg. (2 lbs.) southern-style hash browns
1 tsp. onion salt or 1 medium onion, chopped
garlic and herb seasoning to taste
salt and pepper to taste
6–8 eggs, scrambled
½–1 cup milk
1 (8 oz.) can mushrooms, drained

Cook sausage and remove from Dutch oven. Melt butter in Dutch oven and cook hash browns. Add sausage back in with hash browns, along with the onion salt, garlic and herb seasoning, salt, and pepper. In a separate bowl, scramble eggs, milk, salt, pepper, a small amount of garlic and herb seasoning, and mushrooms. Pour egg mixture in with the sausage and hash browns. Cook until eggs are firm.

Dutch oven size: 12"
Total coals: 24
Top coals: 14
Bottom coals: 10

Breads

NO MEAL IS COMPLETE WITHOUT BREAD!

Remember, you can do almost anything you want to customize these recipes. You can omit or add spices, nuts, cheeses, and so forth to make the bread to your liking. If you don't want to use frozen rolls or bread dough, make your own from scratch!

For easy removal, line your Dutch oven with foil and lightly spray the foil with cooking spray. When your bread is done, just pull the foil out and you'll have hot, fresh bread.

Remember to have more coals on the top of your Dutch oven than you do on the bottom. (See Basic Coal Chart on page 3.) You want your bread to bake from the top down. If you have too much heat on the bottom, your bread will burn.

★ Garlic Rolls ★

20–24 frozen dinner rolls, thawed
½ cube butter or margarine, melted
1½ Tbsp. garlic powder
1 cup mozzarella cheese, grated

Line 14-inch Dutch oven with foil and lightly spray the foil with cooking spray. Place frozen dinner rolls in Dutch oven about ½ to 1 inch apart. Let rise to double in size. Set Dutch oven in warm or sunny place. Drizzle melted butter and garlic powder mixture over top of rolls. With corner of a paper towel, lightly spread the garlic butter on all the rolls. Don't put any pressure on the rolls as you do this. Bake about 10 to 15 minutes or until golden brown on top. Sprinkle cheese on rolls about 5 minutes before rolls are done.

Dutch oven size: 14"
Total coals: 28
Top coals: 18
Bottom coals: 10

★ Variety: Omit garlic and add any kind of cheese or herb.

★ Sasha Clendenin won first place at a Dutch oven cook off. She was
18 years old. You can learn many things from your children.

★ Cinnamon Sugar Rolls ★

20–24 frozen dinner rolls, thawed
½–2 Tbsp. butter, melted
½ cup sugar
3 Tbsp. cinnamon

Line 14-inch Dutch oven with foil and lightly spray the foil with cooking spray. Place dinner rolls in Dutch oven and let rise until doubled in size. Melt butter. Lightly brush butter on rolls, or drizzle it on and use a corner of a paper towel to lightly spread it over all the rolls. (Don't put any pressure on the rolls as you do this.) Combine sugar and cinnamon in a small bowl. Mix well. Sprinkle cinnamon sugar over top of rolls as evenly as possible. Bake for the time it says on the frozen roll bag, or 10 to 15 minutes, or until rolls are golden brown.

Dutch oven size: 14"
Total coals: 28
Top coals: 18
Bottom coals: 10

★ Dinner Rolls ★

20–24 frozen dinner rolls, thawed
2 Tbsp. butter, melted

Line 14-inch Dutch oven with foil and lightly spray the foil with cooking spray. Place frozen dinner rolls in Dutch oven and let rise until doubled in size. Drizzle a small amount of butter over the top of the rolls. With a paper towel, lightly spread the butter so that it runs in between the rolls. Bake for 10 to 15 minutes or until golden brown on top.

Dutch oven size: 14"
Total coals: 28
Top coals: 18
Bottom coals: 10

★ CHeeSe Bread ★

1 loaf frozen bread dough, thawed
¼ cup butter, melted
½–1 cup cheese (any kind), grated

ROLL thawed bread dough out to about ¼-inch thick. Sprinkle on grated cheese and then roll up and seal. Brush bread with butter and place in Dutch oven, seam side down. Let rise until doubled in size. Bake 25–30 minutes or until golden brown.

DUTCH OVEN SIZE: 10"
TOTAL COALS: 20
TOP COALS: 14
BOTTOM COALS: 6

★ To make cleanup easier, you can line the Dutch oven with foil. Just remember to spray the foil with cooking spray so the bread doesn't stick!

★ Breadsticks ★

12 frozen dinner rolls, thawed
4 Tbsp. butter, melted
Parmesan cheese, grated

ROLL thawed dough into sticks about 6 inches long. If desired, cut in half for shorter and thinner breadsticks. Place breadsticks in Dutch oven and let rise until doubled in size. Drizzle a little butter over the top and bake until golden brown. Sprinkle with Parmesan cheese.

DUTCH OVEN SIZE: 12"
TOTAL COALS: 24
TOP COALS: 17
BOTTOM COALS: 7

★ Replace Parmesan cheese with one or more of the following: any other kind of grated cheese, rosemary, parsley flakes, garlic powder, garlic butter, or cinnamon and sugar. If adding grated cheese, sprinkle it on during the last 5 minutes.

★ Apple Pie (Sugar-Free) ★

1 (12-inch) unbaked Dutch oven piecrust (double recipe on page 26)
7–8 cups granny smith apples, peeled, cored, and sliced
1 tsp. cinnamon
1 tsp. nutmeg
¾ cup Splenda, granulated (or sugar)
¾ cup cornstarch
2 Tbsp. butter

PEEL, core, and slice apples in a mixing bowl. Add cinnamon, nutmeg, sugar, and cornstarch. Mix well. Pour apples into Dutch oven piecrust. Dot with butter. Place top crust on and seal. Cut slits in top of crust before baking. Bake at 350 degrees for about 1 hour or until crust is golden brown. Line the Dutch oven with foil and lightly spray the foil with cooking spray so the pie can be lifted out.

DUTCH OVEN SIZE: 12"
TOTAL COALS: 24
TOP COALS: 17
BOTTOM COALS: 7

★ For a faster apple pie, use canned apple pie filling. It will take about 5 to 6 cans of pie filling. For a little variety, drizzle caramel syrup over apples before putting top crust on, or drizzle caramel syrup over top of the pie before or after baking.

★ Berry, Berry, Berry Pie (Sugar-Free) ★

1 (12-inch) unbaked Dutch oven piecrust (double recipe)
1 (1 lb.) bag frozen strawberries
1 (1 lb.) bag frozen raspberries
1 (1 lb.) bag frozen black berries
1 cup Splenda, granulated (or sugar)
½ cup cornstarch

COMBINE all ingredients in a bowl. Mix well. Pour into prepared piecrust. Bake at 350 degrees for 60 minutes or until crust is golden brown.

DUTCH OVEN SIZE: 12"
TOTAL COALS: 24
TOP COALS: 17
BOTTOM COALS: 7

★ Lemon Meringue Pie (Sugar-Free) ★

1 (12-inch) prebaked Dutch oven piecrust (double recipe)
2 large pkg. lemon pudding (cook and serve)
1⅔ cups Splenda, granulated (or sugar)
1 cup lemon juice
6 egg yolks, save egg whites
5 cups water (or 4 cups water and 1 cup lemon juice)

In a medium saucepan, mix lemon pudding, Splenda (or sugar), lemon juice, egg yolks, and water. Stirring constantly, heat on medium heat until mixture reaches a full boil. Cool 5 minutes, stirring twice. Pour into a prebaked 12-inch Dutch oven piecrust.

Dutch oven size: 12"
Total coals: 24
Top coals: 16
Bottom coals: 8

Meringue

6 egg whites
⅓–⅔ cup Splenda, granulated (or sugar)

In a large bowl beat egg whites until stiff. Slowly add Splenda (or sugar) and beat until stiff peaks form when you lift the beaters. Pour on top of the lemon pie and spread evenly, forming peaks as you spread the meringue. Bake for 15–20 minutes or until golden brown. (Don't over-bake! Sometimes the meringue will not turn golden brown in a Dutch oven.) Use 17–18 coals on the top on the outer edge of the lid. For a lighter lemon taste, omit some of the lemon juice and add water. For a stronger lemon taste, add more lemon and less water.

★ Lite Cherry Pie (Sugar-Free) ★

1 (12-inch) unbaked Dutch oven piecrust (double recipe)
3–4 (28 oz. or larger) cans cherry pie filling
1 Tbsp. flour or tapioca (per can of pie filling)
1 tsp. almond extract (per can of pie filling)

POUR pie filling in large bowl. Add flour (or tapioca) and almond extract and mix well. Pour pie filling into prepared Dutch oven piecrust. Top with second crust and seal. Cut slits in top of crust. Bake for 50 to 60 minutes at 350 degrees.

DUTCH OVEN SIZE: 12"
TOTAL COALS: 24
TOP COALS: 17
BOTTOM COALS: 7

★ PUMPKIN Pie ★

1 (12-inch) unbaked Dutch oven piecrust
1 (29 oz.) can solid packed pumpkin
4 eggs
1½ cups sugar or 1 cup Splenda For Baking
3 tsp. cinnamon
2 tsp. ginger
1½ tsp. cloves
2 (12 oz.) cans evaporated milk

MIX ingredients in order given. Pour into prepared Dutch oven piecrust. Remember to line the Dutch oven with foil and lightly spray the foil with cooking spray. Bake for 15 minutes at 450 degrees. Reduce heat to 350 degrees and bake for remaining 50 minutes. (Variation: It can also be baked at 350 degrees for 1 hour or until a knife comes out clean.) Let cool completely and top with whipped cream.

DUTCH OVEN SIZE: 12"

450 DEGREES (FIRST 15 MINUTES)	350 DEGREES (LAST 50 MINUTES)
Total coals: 29	Totals coals: 24
Top coals: 19	Top coals: 17
Bottom coals: 10	Bottom coals: 7

★ Red aNd GOLd ★

1 (21 oz.) can cherry pie filling
1 (8 to 12 oz.) can crushed pineapple, drained
1 box white or yellow cake mix

POUR cherry pie filling and drained pineapple in Dutch oven. Add dry cake mix and stir until well blended. Bake for 45 minutes or until cake is golden brown. Serve warm, topped with whipped cream or ice cream.

DUTCH OVEN SIZE: 10"
TOTAL COALS: 20
TOP COALS: 12
BOTTOM COALS: 8

★ Try any kind of pie filling and fruit. Just remember to have one can pie filling and one regular canned fruit.

★ SODa CObbLEr ★

2 (21 oz.) cans fruit (any kind), drained
1 box white or yellow cake mix
1 (12 oz.) can Sprite or any kind of soda

POUR drained fruit in bottom of Dutch oven. Sprinkle dry cake mix over fruit. Slowly and as evenly as possible pour soda over dry cake mix. Bake 30–40 minutes.

DUTCH OVEN SIZE: 12"
TOTAL COALS: 24
TOP COALS: 16
BOTTOM COALS: 8

★ Fruit Juice Cobbler ★

2 (21 oz.) cans fruit (any kind), drained—reserve juice
½ cup nuts
1 box white or yellow cake mix
1½ cups reserved fruit juice

DRAIN juice from fruit and save juice. Pour drained fruit into Dutch oven. Sprinkle nuts over fruit and sprinkle dry cake mix as evenly as possible over fruit. Drizzle fruit juice as evenly as possible over dry cake mix. Bake 30–40 minutes.

DUTCH OVEN SIZE: 12"
TOTAL COALS: 24
TOP COALS: 18
BOTTOM COALS: 6

★ Lemon Pear Cobbler ★

2–4 (21 oz.) cans pears, diced and drained—reserve juice
½ cup lemon juice
1 box lemon cake mix

DRAIN juice off pears and set juice aside. Pour drained pears into a 12-inch Dutch oven and drizzle about ¼ cup of the lemon juice over pears. Sprinkle dry cake mix as evenly as possible over pears. Drizzle the rest of the lemon juice over the dry cake mix. Drizzle about ¾ cup of the saved pear juice over the dry cake mix. Bake for 30–35 minutes. This cake can be baked in a 9x13 cake pan. Bake for 350 degrees in your home oven for the same amount of time.

DUTCH OVEN SIZE: 12"
TOTAL COALS: 24
TOP COALS: 16
BOTTOM COALS: 8

★ Peach Spice Cobbler ★

. . . .

2 (29 oz.) cans peaches, sliced and drained—reserve juice
1 box spice cake mix
⅔ cup walnuts, chopped (optional)
1 (12 oz.) can Sprite or other soda or fruit juice

SPRAY 12-inch Dutch oven. Pour drained peaches into Dutch oven and drizzle a small amount of peach juice on top. Sprinkle dry cake mix over peaches. Sprinkle walnuts on top. Pour soda over dry cake mix. Bake 35–40 minutes. Serve hot or warm and top with whipped cream.

DUTCH OVEN SIZE: 12"
TOTAL COALS: 24
TOP COALS: 18
BOTTOM COALS: 6

. . . .

★ Add more fruit if desired, or try different fruits and cake mixes.

★ Cherry Nut Spice Cake ★

2 (21 oz.) cans cherry pie filling (or more if desired)
2 tsp. almond extract (or 1 tsp. per can of pie filling)
1 box spice cake mix
½ cup nuts (any kind), chopped

LINE 12-inch Dutch oven with foil and lightly spray the foil with cooking spray. Pour pie filling in Dutch oven. Add almond extract and stir lightly. Mix cake as directed on package and pour it as evenly as possible over the pie filling. Sprinkle nuts on top of cake. (Nuts can also be sprinkled on the pie filling if desired.)

BAKE 50–55 minutes or until a toothpick inserted in the middle comes out clean. Dump cake onto a lined 16-inch pizza pan. Cherries will fall down over the sides of the cake. Add more cherries if desired. Top with whipped cream or ice cream.

DUTCH OVEN SIZE: 12"
TOTAL COALS: 24
TOP COALS: 16
BOTTOM COALS: 8

★ Try any kind of pie filling or any kind of cake mix.

★ Chocolate Peach Upside Down Cake ★

2–3 Tbsp. butter
⅓ cup brown sugar
1 (21 oz.) can peaches, sliced
1½ tsp. cinnamon
½ cup nuts (any kind), chopped
1 tsp. nutmeg
1 box chocolate mix

LINE and spray a 12-inch Dutch oven. Melt butter and add brown sugar. Stir until sugar is dissolved, and then spread around the bottom of the Dutch oven. Place peach slices around Dutch oven. Mix cake according to directions on box and add cinnamon, nuts, and nutmeg to the cake mix. Slowly and carefully pour cake over peaches. Bake for 35–40 minutes or until cake is done. Top with whipped cream or ice cream. This cake is best when it sits overnight or at least cools for about 3–4 hours.

DUTCH OVEN SIZE: 12"
TOTAL COALS: 24
TOP COALS: 18
BOTTOM COALS: 6

★ Coffee Cake ★

....

1 box white or yellow cake mix
1 tsp. cinnamon
1 tsp. nutmeg

Topping:

⅓ cup brown sugar
1½ Tbsp. cinnamon
2 tsp. nutmeg

Mix cake as directed on package. Add cinnamon and nutmeg. Line 10-inch Dutch oven with foil and lightly spray foil with cooking spray. Pour cake into Dutch oven.

Mix topping in order given. Sprinkle on top of cake batter. Cut topping into cake by cutting across batter 2 to 3 times with a knife. Bake 40–45 minutes or until toothpick inserted into cake comes out clean. Use low to medium heat. Don't bake too long or brown sugar could burn. Let cake cool and top with whipped cream and caramel syrup, or you can eat it plain.

Dutch oven size: 10"
Total coals: 20
Top coals: 18
Bottom coals: 6

★ PUMPKiN Spice Cake ★

1 box spice cake
3 eggs
¼ cup oil
¾ cup water

FiLLiNg

1 (29 oz.) can pumpkin
⅔ cup evaporated milk
3 eggs
3 tsp. cinnamon
2 tsp. ginger
1½ tsp. cloves
¾–1 cup Splenda For Baking

MIX cake ingredients in order given and mix well. Line a 12-inch Dutch oven with foil and lightly spray the foil with cooking spray. Pour cake into Dutch oven. Combine the filling ingredients in order given and mix well. Spoon filling onto the cake, leaving about 1 inch of the cake showing all the way around the edges of the Dutch oven. Bake at 350 degrees for 1 hour.

DUTCH OVEN SIZE: 12"
TOTAL COAL: 24
TOP ⌐ S: 18
ʳ   , COALS: 6

6

ONe pot Meals

Add as much or as little to these recipes as you would like. If you add a lot, then you might have to use a bigger Dutch oven, and if you use a bigger Dutch oven, you will need to increase the cooking time and the number of coals. To maintain the cooking temperature, you must put on new coals every 30 to 35 minutes. If you don't, the temperature will drop, and it will take longer for the dish to cook. It also might not turn out the way it should. When we say total coals, that is for each time you put on new coals. If you go to a bigger Dutch oven, refer to the Basic Coal Chart on pages 3 and 4.

★ Lasagna ★

1–2 lbs. lean ground beef
1½ tsp. oil
1 large onion, chopped
1 clove garlic, minced
1 large green bell pepper, chopped
2 (8 oz. or larger) cans mushrooms, drained (optional)
1 qt. canned tomatoes
4 (8 oz.) cans tomato sauce
1 tsp. salt
½ tsp. pepper
¾ tsp. basil
2 lbs. cottage cheese
1 lb. box lasagna noodles
2 lbs. mozzarella cheese, grated

BROWN ground beef in a 14-inch Dutch oven. Remove meat from oven and drain grease. Add oil and sauté vegetables until tender. Add tomatoes, tomato sauce, spices, and meat. Simmer 10 to 15 minutes. Stir cottage cheese into meat mixture. Remove all but two cups of meat mixture. Add a layer of noodles (push noodles into sauce), mozzarella cheese, and a layer of sauce (about 2 cups). Repeat and make four layers each of sauce, noodles, and cheese until everything is gone. End with a layer of cheese. Bake at 350 degrees. Rotate over a quarter turn every 15 minutes for even baking. Let sand about 10 minutes before serving.

DUTCH OVEN SIZE: 14"
TOTAL COALS: 28
TOP COALS: 18
BOTTOM COALS: 10

★ Rebeca Clendenin placed at a Dutch oven
cook off when she was 16 years old.

★ ENCHILADAS ★

1–2 lbs. ground beef
½ medium onion, chopped
½ green bell pepper, chopped
1½ tsp. basil flakes
1½ tsp. Southwest Sizzle Seasoning (optional)
1 pkg. enchilada sauce mix (mix as directed on package)
1 (10-count) pkg. four tortilla shells
1½–2 lbs. cheese (any kind), shredded
1 medium-sized jar salsa (any kind) (optional)
1 (8 oz. or larger) sour cream

BROWN ground beef in cast iron skillet. Add onions, green peppers, basil flakes, and Southwest Sizzle Seasoning. Add a little water and simmer for about 5 minutes. In a cast iron sauce pan, mix enchilada sauce as directed on package. Add about ¼ sauce to the meat and stir. In center of tortilla shell put 1 teaspoon sauce and spread. Add 2–3 tablespoons of meat and cheese (desired amount) in each tortilla and roll and place them in the Dutch oven. All 10 enchiladas can fit in a 14-inch Dutch oven. Pour the remaining sauce over the top of the enchiladas and top with the remaining cheese. Bake for about 30 minutes or until cheese on top is browning. Top with salsa and sour cream.

DUTCH OVEN SIZE: 14"
TOTAL COALS: 28
TOP COALS: 18
BOTTOM COALS: 10

★ BeeF Stew ★

1½ lbs. ground beef or stew meat
4 lbs. potatoes, washed and cut into ½-inch cubes
1 (1 lb.) bag baby carrots
1 medium onion, chopped
1 medium green pepper, chopped
2 (8 oz.) cans mushrooms, drained
1 large can corn, drained
1 large can green beans, drained (optional)
Garlic and pepper seasoning
salt to taste
9 oz. (or more) brown gravy mix

BROWN meat in 12-inch deep Dutch oven and drain grease. Add potatoes, carrots, onions, green peppers, and water to cover. Cook until vegetables are tender. Add mushrooms, corn, green beans, seasoning, and gravy mix. Cook until vegetables are to liking. Add any kind of vegetables desired. If you are adding a lot of vegetables to the stew, the Dutch oven will have to be 14 inches.

DUTCH OVEN SIZE: 12" deep
TOTAL COALS: 24
TOP COALS: 14
BOTTOM COALS: 10

★ Hamburger and Potatoes ★

1 lb. ground beef
½–1 cube butter
3–4 potatoes, washed and diced
1–2 tsp. dehydrated onions (or ½ medium onion, chopped)
1 can corn, drained
1 (8 oz.) can mushrooms, drained
2 tsp. garlic pepper
2 tsp. Southwest Sizzle Seasoning (optional) or any other spice
2 tsp. salt
2 oz. (or more) brown gravy mix (makes 2 cups)

BROWN ground beef and set aside. Melt butter in bottom of Dutch oven and cook potatoes. When potatoes are done, add ground beef, onions, corn, mushrooms, garlic pepper, Southwest Sizzle Seasoning, and salt. Stir everything together well. Stirring often, cook for 15–20 minutes or until everything is heated through. In a sauce pan make brown gravy as directed on package. The gravy can be mixed in or put on as it is served, depending on what you want to do.

DUTCH OVEN SIZE: 12" deep
TOTAL COALS: 24
TOP COALS: 14
BOTTOM COALS: 10

★ Christmas Meadows Chicken and Rice ★

½–1 lb. chicken, diced and cooked
1 box Rice-a-Roni (any kind)
1 can cream soup (any kind)
1 (8 oz.) can mushrooms, drained
vegetable(s) of your choice, if desired

Cook chicken until no longer pink and set aside. Cook Rice-a-Roni as directed on package. Mix soup as directed on can. When almost all the water in the rice has been absorbed, add the soup, chicken, mushrooms, and any other vegetables you desire. Simmer for 5–10 minutes. Stir often to make sure that the rice does not stick to the Dutch oven. This recipe can be done in a large cast iron skillet, cast iron wok, or a Dutch oven.

Dutch oven size: 10"
Total coals: 20
Top coals: 12
Bottom coals: 8

★ This will serve about 4 to 5 people. If you double this recipe you will have to use a big pot when you combine all of the ingredients or if you add other assorted vegetables.

★ Chicken and Vegetable Bake ★

1½ lbs. chicken, diced
1 small onion, chopped (or 1–2 tsp. dehydrated onions)
2 cups cauliflower, chopped (optional)
any other vegetable(s) of your choice, if desired
1 can corn, drained (optional)
2 large cans mushrooms, drained
2 cups instant rice
2 cups water
salt and pepper to taste
Southwest Sizzle Seasoning to taste (optional)

Cook diced chicken and drain grease. Cook chicken a little longer to brown. When chicken is cooked through, set aside. Add onions and any raw vegetables that need to be cooked and sauté until tender. Add salt and pepper, Southwest Sizzle Seasoning, chicken, mushrooms, rice, and water to the vegetables. Cook according to the directions on the rice. If desired, add a cream soup or gravy. If adding soup you can omit some of the water and add the can of soup or gravy.

Dutch oven: 12"
Total coals: 24
Top coals: 14
Bottom coals: 10

5–6 chicken breasts, cut into 1-inch pieces
salt and pepper to taste
garlic and herb seasoning to taste
½ tsp. sweet basil
paprika to taste
Tuscan chicken seasoning to taste
1 (8 oz.) pkg. pasta (any kind), cooked
1 (15 oz.) can corn, drained
2 (8 oz.) cans mushrooms, drained
1 (15 oz.) bag frozen broccoli, thawed
1–2 cups cheese (any kind), shredded (optional)
4 cups herb white sauce (page 53)

CUT up and cook chicken. Add salt, pepper, garlic and herb season-ing, sweet basil, paprika, and Tuscan chicken seasoning. Cook chicken until it starts to turn a golden brown. Remove chicken and place on paper towel to remove excess grease. Cook pasta while cooking the chicken, adding ½ teaspoon salt the pasta water. When pasta is done, drain and return pasta to the Dutch oven. Add chicken, corn, mush-rooms, and broccoli. Mix well and add more spices if needed. Make Herb White Sauce (page 53). Pour the Herb White Sauce over top of chicken and pasta mixture and mix well. Cook until broccoli is tender. Top with cheese and cook until melted. For a different flavor, replace Tuscan chicken seasoning with any kind of chicken seasoning you have or prefer.

DUTCH OVEN SIZE: 12"
TOTAL COALS: 24
TOP COALS: 14
BOTTOM COALS: 10

★ Herb White Sauce ★

8 Tbsp. butter
8 Tbsp. all-purpose flour
4 cups milk
1 tsp. salt
1 tsp. pepper
1 Tbsp. minced onions
1 tsp. garlic and herb seasoning
1 tsp. sweet basil

MELT butter in sauce pan over low heat. Blend in flour with wire whisk and add milk, salt, pepper, minced onions, garlic and herb seasoning, and sweet basil. Stir constantly until mixture bubbles and is thick. Add more spices if desired. Pour over your dish and mix well.

12 chicken tenders, cut into ½-inch pieces
salt and pepper to taste
paprika to taste
garlic and herb seasoning to taste
½–1 tsp. Tuscan chicken seasoning
2–3 cups rice, cooked
1 pkg. frozen broccoli, chopped and thawed
3–4 cups soupy white sauce (page 55)
1 can corn, drained (optional)
¼ tsp. sweet basil (optional)

CUT up and cook chicken tenders in a little oil in a 12-inch Dutch oven. Add salt, pepper, paprika, garlic and herb seasoning, and Tuscan chicken seasoning. Cook until chicken starts to turn golden brown. Meanwhile, cook rice in a separate saucepan. When rice is done, add to chicken. Add broccoli and cook until tender. Meanwhile, make Soupy White Sauce (page 55) in sauce pan. Add corn and basil if desired. Pour Soupy White Sauce over the top of the rice and mix well. Cook for an additional 5–10 minutes or until sauce starts to bubble.

DUTCH OVEN SIZE: 12"
TOTAL COALS: 24
TOP COALS: 14
BOTTOM COALS: 10

★ Soupy White Sauce ★

4 Tbsp. butter, melted
3 cups milk, divided
1 can cream soup (any kind)
4 Tbsp. all-purpose flour
½ tsp. salt
½ tsp. pepper
½ tsp. garlic and herb seasoning
½ sweet basil
1 Tbsp. minced onions

MELT butter in a saucepan. In a separate bowl, mix 1 cup milk and the soup. Add flour to melted butter and then add remaining milk a little at a time. Whisk in soup. Add salt, pepper, garlic and herb seasoning, sweet basil, and minced onion. Mix well. Cook until sauce starts getting thick, and stir often to keep it from burning or sticking to the pan.

★ Christmas Meadows Souper Rice ★

1 box Rice-a-Roni (any kind)
1 can cream soup (any kind)

COOK Rice-a-Roni according to package directions. Mix soup as directed on can. When the water is almost all absorbed into the rice, add the soup and simmer for 5–7 minutes. This will let the soup cook into the rice and allow it to thicken. Add vegetables if desired.

DUTCH OVEN SIZE: 10"
TOTAL COALS: 20
TOP COALS: 12
BOTTOM COALS: 8

★ This recipe can also be done in a cast iron skillet or a cast iron wok.

★ Pork Chop Delight ★

6 pork chops
1 can cream of mushroom soup
1 soup can milk or water
1 (8 oz.) can mushrooms, drained
season to taste

Cook and season pork chops in 12-inch Dutch oven. Mix soup with the water or milk. Add diluted soup and mushrooms to the pork chops and stir. Simmer for 15 to 20 minutes. Potatoes and any other vegetables can be added to this dish.

Dutch oven size: 12"
Total coals: 24
Top coals: 14
Bottom coals: 10

★ Pork Chops and Potatoes ★

3 pork chops, cubed
paprika to taste
2 tsp. garlic and herb seasoning
salt and pepper to taste
1 box Loaded Au Gratin potatoes
1 cup sour cream

Cut up and cook pork chops in a 10-inch Dutch oven. Season with paprika, garlic and herb seasoning, salt, and pepper. Add Au Gratin potatoes and mix according to package directions. Add sour cream and cook for the amount of time listed on the package.

Dutch oven size: 10"
Total coals: 20
Top coals: 12
Bottom coals: 8

★ Roast, Potatoes, and Carrots ★

1 (3–5 lb.) roast
salt and pepper to taste
1 tsp. garlic powder
2 onions, sliced about ¼-inch thick
4–5 potatoes, washed and cut into fourths
1 (16 oz.) bag baby carrots
2 cups water (add more if needed)

PLACE roast in 12-inch Dutch oven with fat side up. Season the roast and place the onion on top. Pour water in around the roast, and add more water if needed. (Make sure there is water in the Dutch oven at all times so the roast doesn't burn.) Cook until 45–50 minutes are left and then add the potatoes and carrots. Add more water (about halfway up the sides) so the vegetables will cook. Continue cooking until vegetables are desired tenderness.

DUTCH OVEN SIZE: 12"
TOTAL COALS: 24
TOP COALS: 14
BOTTOM COALS: 10

★ Remember to put new coals on every 30–35 minutes.

★ Steak and Vegetables ★

London broil steaks (or any kind of steak you prefer)
1–2 cans cream of mushroom soup, diluted
    (or any kind of cream soup)
1–2 (8 oz.) cans mushrooms, drained
1 medium onion, chopped
1 medium green bell pepper, cut into ⅛-inch strips
6 medium potatoes, washed and cut into ¼-inch pieces
1 can corn (optional)
season to taste

Cook steaks and season to taste as desired. Mix soup and 1–2 cans water and pour it over the top of the steaks. Add mushrooms, onions, green peppers, potatoes, corn, and any other vegetable you would like and season to taste. If the soup gets too thick, add a little more water or milk and stir well. Stir often so food will cook evenly.

Dutch oven size: 12"
Total coals: 24
Top coals: 14
Bottom coals: 10

★ Sausage and Hash Browns ★

1 lb. polish sausage, sliced
1 tsp. onion salt (or ½ medium onion, chopped)
1 pkg. hash browns
½ cube butter, melted
1 tsp. garlic and herb seasoning
salt and pepper to taste
1 (8 oz.) can mushrooms

SLICE and cook sausage. Set aside. (If using diced onion, sauté the onion in a little butter before cooking the hash browns.) Cook hash browns in Dutch oven with butter, seasoning with garlic and herb seasoning, salt, pepper, and onion salt. Add more butter if needed. After hash browns are cooked, return sausage to Dutch oven and add mushrooms and more seasoning (if desired). Heat for 5–10 minutes. Add other vegetables if desired.

DUTCH OVEN SIZE: 10"
TOTAL COALS: 20
TOP COALS: 12
BOTTOM COALS: 8

★ Christmas Meadows Vegetable Soup ★

1½–2 lbs. ground beef, cooked
1 (16 oz.) bag frozen corn
1 (16 oz.) bag frozen green beans
1 (16 oz.) bag frozen mixed vegetables
1 (16 oz.) bag baby carrots
6–8 potatoes, diced
1 medium onion, chopped
season to taste
2–3 (8 oz.) cans mushrooms, drained
any other vegetables you desire
water to cover
1–2 bay leaves (optional)
3 pkg. brown gravy mix

Brown ground beef and season. Pour off grease. Add vegetables and enough water to cover. Add bay leaf on top of vegetables. Mix gravy according to package directions and add to beef/vegetable mixture. Season more if needed. Stirring often, cook until potatoes are tender. If desired, add more gravy mix for thicker soup. Remove bay leaf before serving. (Or you can use 1–2 teaspoons basil flakes instead of the bay leaf.)

Dutch oven size: 14"
Total coals: 28
Top coals: 16
Bottom coals: 12

Meats

START WITH A GREAT MEAT DISH

To bring out the natural flavor of any meat, add a bay leaf to your Dutch oven while cooking. Basil will also enhance these natural flavors. If you use a bay leaf, remember to remove it before serving.

The longer you simmer your meat, the more tender it will be. Most of the time, it will just fall apart when you pull it out. It will be so tender that it will almost melt in your mouth!

★ Sloppy Joes ★

2½–4 lbs. lean ground beef
¾ tsp. barbecue sauce seasoning (optional)
1 tsp. garlic salt
pepper to taste
1 tsp. basil flakes
½ medium onion, diced
2 pkg. sloppy joe mix
2 (8 oz.) cans tomato sauce

Brown ground beef and drain grease. Add spices and onions. Cook for 15–20 minutes. Add sloppy joe mix, tomato sauce, and water as directed on package. Cook 45–90 minutes, depending on the amount of meat used (see table below).

For 2½ lbs.:	For 4 lbs. or More:
Cook 45 minutes	Cook 90 minutes
Dutch oven size: 12"	Dutch oven size: 14"
Total coals: 24	Total coals: 28
Top coals: 14	Top coals: 16
Bottom coals: 10	Bottom coals: 12

★ Bottled barbecue sauce can also be used, or try your own sloppy joe recipe!

★ Basic Meatloaf ★

2½–5 lbs. lean ground beef
½–1 large onion, chopped
2 medium carrots, chopped
½–1 medium green bell pepper, chopped (optional)
garlic pepper seasoning salt to taste
1 (8 oz.) can tomato sauce
½ cup barbecue sauce
⅛ to ¼ cup all-purpose flour
1 egg
1–2 (8 oz.) cans mushrooms, drained

Combine all ingredients together. Mix with your hands until everything is combined well. Shape into a loaf or in the shape of the bowl you are using and put into Dutch oven.

For 2½ lbs.:	For 5 lbs.:
Dutch oven size: 12"	Dutch oven size: 14"
Total coals: 24	Total coals: 28
Top coals: 14	Top coals: 16
Bottom coals: 10	Bottom coals: 12

★ Be sure to wash your hands well before and after you mix the meatloaf.

★ Two Meat Barbecue ★

12 country style pork ribs
12 chicken breasts (or 18 tenders)
1 (32 oz.) bottle barbecue sauce (any kind)
season to taste

In a 12-inch Dutch oven, season pork ribs and cook until done. Remove pork ribs and set aside. Remove liquid and put chicken in Dutch oven. Season and cook until done. Pour out liquid and put all meat back in Dutch oven. Add the barbecue sauce. (You can add more barbecue sauce if you want.) Simmer for 45 minutes or longer. The longer it simmers, the more sauce will be absorbed into the meat. The meat should be very tender.

Dutch oven size: 14"
Total coals: 28
Top coals: 16
Bottom coals: 12

★ Try replacing the pork ribs with beef ribs, or use all three meats!

★ Ribs and Chicken ★

5 boneless pork ribs, cubed
5 boneless skinless chicken breasts, cubed
salt and pepper to taste
1 tsp. sweet basil
1½ tsp. garlic and herb seasoning
1 Tbsp. minced onion
½ bottle barbecue sauce (any kind)

CUT up and cook pork ribs and chicken separately. Drain grease or liquid. When both pork ribs and chicken are done, place both back into Dutch oven. Add salt, pepper, sweet basil, garlic and herb seasoning, and minced onions. Stir well. Add barbecue sauce. Simmer for about 20 minutes or longer. The longer it simmers, the more tender the meat well be.

DUTCH OVEN SIZE: 12"
TOTAL COALS: 24
TOP COALS: 14
BOTTOM COALS: 10

★ Dutch Oven Ham ★

5 lbs. ham
⅛ tsp. garlic powder
½ tsp. basil flakes
2 (¼-inch) slices onion
2 cups (or more) water

PLACE ham in a 12-inch Dutch oven. Sprinkle with garlic powder and basil flakes and place onion slices on top. Carefully pour water over the ham. Bake about 2 hours. Don't let the ham dry out. Check it about every 30 minutes and add more water if needed.

DUTCH OVEN SIZE: 12"
TOTAL COALS: 24
TOP COALS: 14
BOTTOM COALS: 10

★ Chicken in Sauce ★

6 boneless skinless chicken breasts (or 1½–2 lbs. chicken tenders)
season to taste
1 medium bottle barbecue sauce (any kind)

PLACE chicken in 12-inch Dutch oven. Season well with desired seasonings. Cook chicken until it's done. Pour barbecue sauce over chicken and simmer for another 30 minutes (or longer).

DUTCH OVEN SIZE: 12"
TOTAL COALS: 24
TOP COALS: 14
BOTTOM COALS: 10

Try the chicken without the barbecue sauce and just season it well. We like boneless and skinless chicken, but bone-in chicken can also be used.

Don't be a chicken—try cooking chicken in a Dutch oven!

★ Roast ★

3–5 lbs. roast
garlic salt and pepper to taste
2 (¼-inch) slices onion
2 cups water

PLACE roast in Dutch oven. Season the roast and place the onion slices on top. Carefully pour the water in. Cook according to times listed in table below (depending on the amount of meat used).

	For 3 lbs.:	For 5 lbs.:
COOKING TIME	2 to 2½ hours	3½ to 4 hours
DUTCH OVEN SIZE	10"	12"
TOTAL COALS	20	24
TOP COALS	12	14
BOTTOM COALS	8	10

★ Marinade For Roast ★

¾ cup water
1 oz. brown gravy mix
½ tsp. steak seasoning
½ tsp. garlic powder
¼ tsp. onion salt
¼ tsp. paprika
¼ tsp. black pepper
⅛ tsp. salt

COMBINE all ingredients as given. Mix well and inject into roast. Pour extra over top and cook.

★ BBQ Ribs ★

1–2 (family size) pkg. pork or beef ribs
season to taste
1 large bottle barbecue sauce

SEASON and cook ribs. Drain grease. Pour barbecue sauce over the ribs and simmer for at least 30 minutes. Cook to your liking, but remember pork must be fully cooked.

DUTCH OVEN SIZE: 12"
TOTAL COALS: 24
TOP COALS: 14
BOTTOM COALS: 10

★ We prefer the pork ribs. Try them without the
barbecue sauce and just season them well.

★ MOM'S BBQ Sauce ★

1 (8oz.) can tomato sauce
½ cup water
¼ cup vinegar
2 Tbsp. sugar
1 tsp. chili powder
⅛ tsp. pepper
⅛ tsp. salt
dash cayenne pepper
1 Tbsp. dried onion (or ¼ medium onion, chopped)
¼ medium green bell pepper, chopped
½ tsp. basil flakes

COMBINE all ingredients in saucepan. Stir well and heat on high until sauce comes to a boil. Simmer until thick. Makes about 1½ cups.

★ This recipe can be used on any of the recipes that call for barbecue sauce.
It is a recipe that our mother made for her Sloppy Joes or BBQ beef.

★ Spicy Meatloaf ★

5 lbs. ground beef
2 (8 oz.) cans mushrooms, drained
1 (8 oz.) can tomato sauce
1 medium onion, chopped
1 medium green bell pepper, chopped
½ lb. bag baby carrots, chopped
2 eggs
2 tsp. basil flakes
2 tsp. minced garlic
2–3 tsp. Southwest Sizzle Seasoning (optional)
1 tsp. salt
1 tsp. pepper
4 Tbsp. parsley flakes
½ cup bread crumbs
2 cups cheese (any kind) shredded and divided

SET aside 1 cup cheese and combine the rest of the ingredients in a large bowl. Mix with hands until everything is well combined. Form mixture into a loaf or bowl shape and put into Dutch oven. Sprinkle reserved cheese on top. Cook 2½–3 hours.

DUTCH OVEN SIZE: 14"
TOTAL COALS: 28
TOP COALS: 16
BOTTOM COALS: 12

★ If you don't have bread crumbs, use corn flakes, flour, or oatmeal.

★ Herb Meatloaf ★

5–6 lbs. ground beef
½ tsp. chives
¾ tsp. garlic powder
¾ tsp. rosemary
2 tsp. Southwest Seasoning
½ medium onion, chopped (or 2 tsp. onion flakes)
2 eggs
1 cup oatmeal
1 tsp. salt
1 tsp. pepper
1 cup cheese (any kind)
12 crackers (like Ritz or saltines), crushed
¼ cup carrots, shredded

Add ingredients as given and mix well with your hands. Heat oven to 350 degrees. Cook for about 2 hours or until cooked through.

Dutch oven size: 12" deep
Total coals: 24
Top coals: 14
Bottom coals: 10

Side Dishes

COMPLETE YOUR MEAL WITH A TASTY SIDE DISH!

No meal is complete without a side dish. We especially love to try different types of potato dishes. It is fun to just throw a variety of ingredients into a Dutch oven and have it turn out the way we wanted it to. The recipe for baked beans is the first one we ever tried in a Dutch oven. Try anything you like and see if you can create a recipe of your own. You don't always have to stay on the "safe side" by just cooking basic stews or soups. If you do, you'll miss out on a lot of great food!

B & S Potatoes

1½–2 lbs. southern-style hash browns
½ medium onion, chopped
2 cans cream soup (any kind)
½ cup water or milk
1 (8 oz.) sour cream
salt and pepper to taste
1 lb. cheese (any kind), grated

BROWN potatoes and onions. Add soup, water, sour cream, salt, and pepper. Add cheese to top. Mix well. Cook 45 minutes.

DUTCH OVEN SIZE: 12"
TOTAL COALS: 24
TOP COALS: 16
BOTTOM COALS: 8

High Country Hash Browns

½ lb. bacon, cut into 1-inch strips
½ medium onion, chopped
1–1½ lbs. hash browns
½–1 cube butter
season to taste

COOK bacon until crisp. Set aside and drain grease, leaving 1–2 teaspoons in Dutch oven. Sauté onions in bacon grease until tender. Set aside with bacon. Cook hash browns and season to taste. When hash browns are done, add bacon and onions. Stir well and let cook for a few more minutes. This can also be done in the cast iron skillet.

DUTCH OVEN SIZE: 10"
TOTAL COALS: 20
TOP COALS: 13
BOTTOM COALS: 7

CreaMier Potatoes

....

1 (2 lb.) bag southern-style hash browns
½ medium onion, chopped
½ green pepper, chopped
1 (8 oz.) can mushrooms, drained
1 cup milk
2 cans cream soup (any kind)
1 (8 oz.) sour cream
salt and pepper to taste
3 cups cheese (any kind), grated and divided

SPRAY 12-inch Dutch oven and pour in hash browns. Add onions, green peppers, mushrooms, milk, soup, sour cream, seasoning, and 1½ cups cheese. Mix well. Top with remaining cheese. Cook for 30–35 minutes.

DUTCH OVEN SIZE: 12"
TOTAL COALS: 24
TOP COALS: 15
BOTTOM COALS: 9

Baked Beans

1 lb. bacon
1 lb. ground beef (optional)
1 medium onion, chopped
1 medium green bell pepper, chopped
1 can lima beans, drained
1 can garbanzo beans, drained
1 can red beans, drained
1 can pinto beans, drained
1 can pork and beans
¾ cup ketchup
¾ cup brown sugar
2½ tsp. vinegar
1½ tsp. salt
2 tsp. mustard

Cook bacon and crumble it or cut it into 1-inch pieces. Drain grease. Cook ground beef, onions, and green peppers until ground beef is brown and vegetables are tender. Drain grease. Add bacon back in and then add all the beans. Add remaining ingredients and mix well. Cook for 40–45 minutes.

DUTCH OVEN SIZE: 12"
TOTAL COALS: 24
TOP COALS: 14
BOTTOM COALS: 10

★ Try sausage or diced ham instead of the ground beef.
Add more onion and green bell pepper if desired.

CLaM CHoWder SouP

....

4 cups potatoes, cubed
2 Tbsp. minced onions (or 1 medium onion, chopped)
2 tsp. celery salt (or 1 cup celery, chopped)
2 tsp. sweet basil
2 cans minced clams, drained—reserve juice
¾ cup butter, melted
¾ cup all-purpose flour
4 cups milk
1 (8 oz.) can mushrooms, drained
1 (15 oz.) can corn, drained
1 tsp. salt
1 tsp. pepper
3 tsp. garlic and herb seasoning

WASH, peel (optional), and cut potatoes. Place in sauce pan and add minced onion, celery salt, sweet basil, and any other desired raw vegetables. Add saved clam juice and enough water to barely cover the vegetables. Bring to a simmer. Meanwhile, in a 12-inch Dutch oven, melt butter over low heat. Using a wire whisk, add flour and milk. Cook until thick. Add potato mixture (including liquid), mushrooms, corn, salt, pepper, garlic and herb seasoning, and clams. Stir well. Bring to a boil and cook for 20–30 minutes. Stir every 10 minutes or so.

DUTCH OVEN SIZE: 10"
TOTAL COALS: 8 (bottom only)

AboUt tHe AUtHorS

Lynn Child & Susan Clendenin

Lynn Child is the sixth child of Eldon and Leona Butler Child. He is retired and has many hobbies. He is not married. Lynn loves to go fishing and camping. He also likes to take care of his yard and his many rosebushes and to work in his wood shop.

Susan Gale Child Clendenin is the eighth child of Eldon and Leona Butler Child. She is married and has one stepdaughter, one stepson, and two stepgrandsons. She and her husband also have two daughters—Sasha, who is twenty, and Rebeca, who is eighteen.

Susan has many hobbies. Her family likes to do things outdoors. She works for the school transportation department in an area close to where she and her family live.

Lynn and Susan's family do a lot of things together, like camping, and Susan's husband goes fishing with Lynn. Of course, they love to do Dutch oven cooking together and to be themselves as much as they can and anywhere they can.

0 26575 09639 2